THE SINGING CHAMELEON

By the same Author

The Long Grass Whispers
Where the Leopard Passes
The Hunter's Cave

THE SINGING CHAMELEON

A Book of African Stories
based on local Custom, Proverbs
and Folk-lore

by

GERALDINE ELLIOT

ILLUSTRATED BY SHEILA HAWKINS

Routledge & Kegan Paul
London and Henley

First published in 1957
by Routledge & Kegan Paul Ltd
39 Store Street,
London WC1E 7DD and
Broadway House,
Newtown Road,
Henley-on-Thames,
Oxon RG9 1EN

Reprinted 1962, 1971, 1981

ISBN 0 7100 0862 7

Printed in Hong Kong

Now both parents had to work to feed the babies. They hunted for long hours over the park and cemetery to find small animals to carry back to the nest. With their sharp beaks, they tore off scraps of meat and gently gave them to the chicks. The one that had hatched first was the biggest – he was older than the others – and he usually managed to get the main helping of mice and beetles that his parents brought back. The second baby got the next share, while the third sometimes went hungry. But he was lucky, for there were a lot of mice about. Otherwise, he might have starved, because the stronger chicks are always fed first.

For five weeks both parents brought food to the nest hole to feed their hungry family. As the chicks grew, their feathers began to push through the down that covered them, until they looked much like their parents and were nearly as big. Then, one warm night in late May, the biggest chick climbed to the entrance of the nest hole and glided down to the ground. Within a week, all three had left the nursery.

Yet although they could fly and see and hear as well as their parents, the young owls had a lot to learn. At first they caught hardly anything, but their parents were at hand, and continued to feed them. By now the babies did not need to have a mouse cut up, but grabbed it and swallowed it whole as soon as one of the adults appeared with it. When the old birds were not about, they tried to hunt for themselves. Sometimes they succeeded in catching a mouse or a vole which was as inexperienced as they were. But to begin with, that was all.

During the summer, the owlets learned many things. They improved as hunters, so that although they still missed some mice, they caught quite a lot for themselves. They learned about the town, and the best places to roost and feed, and they learned about some of their enemies, such as cats and traffic.

Then as the days grew shorter and the nights longer, there were fewer mice and insects and the parent owls needed all they could catch to keep themselves alive. In any case, the baby birds were now fully grown and could hunt quite well, so the adults no longer fed them. Soon, if the chicks

approached their mother, she no longer offered them food, but clattered her beak in warning. They knew that their days of being cared for were over. Before the winter, they flew away towards the suburbs, where they found shelter and food in the gardens of new housing estates.

Even the owl and her mate did not remain together although on frosty nights they still called to each other as they hunted in their separate parts of the town. But next spring they would come together again to raise a new family.

Everything in this book is true. Owls live in many towns, hunting for mice and small birds and insects. Listen at night for their calls. They make a long, wavering hoot, or a sharp 'kee-wick' sound. If you can imitate an owl, you will find that a real owl will often answer your call.

Another way of studying owls is to discover a place where an owl roosts. Nearby you will find the pellets the owl produces as it digests its food. These pellets are not unpleasant or dangerous to handle, and by taking them apart very carefully you will be able to see the remains of the creatures that the owl has been feeding on.

Animal remains you might find in an owl pellet.

An owl feather

You can put up a big nest-box for owls in your garden ➧